Mojito Recipe That Will Exceed Your Expectations

Prepare the Best Mojitos with This Recipe Book

BY: Nancy Silverman

COPYRIGHT NOTICES

© 2020 Nancy Silverman All Rights Reserved

Subject to the agreement and permission of the author, this Book, in part or in whole, may not be reproduced in any format. This includes but is not limited to electronically, in print, scanning or photocopying.

The opinions, guidelines and suggestions written here are solely those of the Author and are for information purposes only. Every possible measure has been taken by the Author to ensure accuracy but let the Reader be advised that they assume all risk when following information. The Author does not assume any risk in the case of damages, personally or commercially, in the case of misinterpretation or misunderstanding while following any part of the Book.

Table of Contents

Introduction 6

Original Cuban mojito recipe 8

Mojito for a crowd 11

Blueberry mojito 13

Tropical coconut mojito recipe 15

Bloody orange mojito recipe 17

Mexican mojito with strawberry 19

Pomegranate mojito cocktail recipe 21

Summer watermelon mojito 23

Refreshing raspberry mojito 26

Pina colada mojito 29

Alcohol-free virgin mojito 31

Vodka mojito 33

Red mojito 35

Frozen coconut mojito 37

Low carb mojito recipe 39

Red vodka mojito 41

Green tea mojito 43

Summer peach mojito 45

Italian Limoncello mojito 47

Cherry lime mojito recipe 49

Lavender lemonade mojito recipe 51

Mojito sangria 54

Frozen mojito with passion fruit 56

Watermelon mojito popsicles 58

Refreshing blackberry mojito popsicles 60

Strawberry mojito popsicles 62

Easy kiwi mojito popsicles 64

Coconut mojito popsicles 66

Frozen mojito slushie 69

Alcohol-free watermelon mojito slushie 71

Conclusion 73

About the Author 75

Author's Afterthoughts 77

Introduction

Do you know what it takes to prepare the best mojito ever? This Mojito Recipe Book will reveal all the hidden tips and tricks to you. Once you have it in your hands, you will know that this is the deal for you.

The art of cocktail making is revealed through the pages of the Mojito Recipe Book. You don't need to have special skills at all. All you need are these precise recipes with clear instructions. Soon, you will have an interesting thing to do on Friday night. You can show off your new skills in front of your friends. They will be amazed for sure!

This recipe book is a good choice for the bar managers that want to make a change. If you find that your bar is not so attractive to customers, you would want to bring new drinks on the menu. They will instantly draw people that want to try something new. Fill your menu with these Instagram-worthy variations of mojito and business will start to grow.

Are you ready to learn the secret tricks behind the best mojito cocktails? Let's get started!

Original Cuban mojito recipe

Not everyone knows the secret behind the original mojito recipe. There is no better way to start this recipe book than sharing the hidden tricks. Many bartenders have made their customized variations. But this recipe will show you how to prepare one original mojito.

The combination of sweet, sour, and the strong flavor of the rum will create an amazing sensation. It will make you feel like you are wandering through the colorful streets of Havana.

Total time: 5 minutes

Servings: 1

Ingredients

- 1 tsp powdered sugar
- Freshly squeezed juice from one lime
- 2 oz white rum
- 4 fresh mint leaves
- 2 oz club soda
- crushed ice
- 1 sprig of mint

Instructions

Add the mint on the bottom of the glass. Use a tall collins glass of this cocktail.

Pour in the lime juice over the mint.

Sprinkle the sugar too. Middle until the ingredients are combined, and the mint has released its flavor.

Add ice. Pour the rum over the ice and finish with club soda. Finish with mint and lime wedge on top.

Mojito for a crowd

Need a drink for a crowd? This mojito pitcher recipe is here to save you. This recipe will give you a precise amount of **Ingredients** for you to make a large batch. All you need to do is present the pitcher on the table, and the guests will be able to refill the glass by themselves. This is perfect for those parties with a large number of people. You won't need to check with everyone to see if their glass is empty and needs to be refilled. Simply put a few of these pitchers and let your guests help themselves!

Total time: 10 minutes

Servings: 6

Ingredients

- 5 limes
- 35 fresh mint leaves
- 1 cup white rum
- 1/2 cup plus 2 tbsp granulated sugar
- 34 oz club soda

Instructions

1. Cut the lime in quarters. Add them into a large pitcher.

2. Add the mint and sugar. Muddle the ingredients until the sugar is dissolved.

3. Pour in the white rum. Mix well until the sugar is completely dissolved.

4. Let the mojito chill in the fridge. When it is ready to serve, pour in the club soda.

5. Serve into glasses filled with ice.

Blueberry mojito

If you want something different, then the blueberry mojito recipe will amaze you. You can be creative with this cocktail and create many versions. But, keep in mind that not all of them work. Not every ingredient will fit the specific flavor. But, be sure that the following one is an excellent match!

Total time: 10 minutes

Servings: 2

Ingredients

- 2 tsp sugar
- 6 oz club soda
- 10 fresh mint leaves
- Freshly squeezed juice of 2 limes
- 1 cup fresh blueberries, plus extra for garnish
- 4 oz white rum
- Crushed ice
- Two lime wedges

Instructions

1. Add the blueberries in a blender. Puree until smooth. Set aside.

2. In a cocktail shaker, add mint and sugar. Muddle until combined.

3. Add the lime juice, the blueberry puree, rum, and shake well.

4. Add ice and club soda in two tall glasses. Pour the cocktail from the mixer. Garnish with blueberries, mint, and lime wedge.

Tropical coconut mojito recipe

If you enjoy sipping a tropical cocktail on a summer night, then you shouldn't miss this recipe. The sour citrus taste is enhanced with the creamy coconut. Both of the flavors create a pleasurable feeling that reminds you of summer vacation. On the other hand, this is an excellent addition to your summer bar menu.

Total time: 5 minutes

Servings: 1

Ingredients

- 8 mint leaves
- Freshly squeezed juice from 1 lime
- 2 tsp. granulated sugar
- 1 oz coconut drink mixer
- 3 oz. white rum
- club soda
- lime wedge for garnish
- Mint for garnish
- coconut flakes for garnish

Instructions

1. Add the mint, sugar, lime juice, and coconut drink mixer into a mojito glass. The coconut drink mixer is special for cocktails, don't mistake it with coconut milk.

2. Use a cocktail muddler or a wooden spoon to twist the mint leaves. Muddle until the aroma is released.

3. Add the white rum. Fill ¾ of the mojito glass with crushed ice.

4. Fill the rest with the club soda. Garnish with mint, lime, and coconut flakes. Enjoy!

Bloody orange mojito recipe

The mojito already has a hint of citrus. But what happens when you add some more? This time try with blood oranges. The sweet note will enhance the cocktail and give it a specific flavor. Plus, it will look so decorative. Don't forget to decorate with a slice on top.

Total time: 10 minutes

Servings: 1

Ingredients

- 6 sprigs of mint + more for garnish
- 1 ounce Blood orange juice, freshly squeezed
- 1 tbsp Lime juice, freshly squeezed
- 1 ounce light rum
- 2 tbsp Simple syrup
- club soda
- Slice of blood orange

Instructions

1. In a tall glass, pour the orange and lime juice. Add in the simple syrup. It is easier to use simple syrup because you don't have to dissolve it as you would do with sugar.

2. Add in the mint leaves. Muddle until they release the aroma.

3. Add the rum. Fill the rest of the glass with club soda. Garnish with a slice of orange and mint.

Mexican mojito with strawberry

What happens when you replace the rum with tequila? You have a nice Mexican mojito. Add some strawberries, and you have the ultimate party cocktail. No one can resist the sweet and sour taste, accompanied with the freshness of the strawberries.

Total time: 10 minutes

Servings: 1

Ingredients

- 1 oz Lime juice
- 4 Mint leaves
- 1 oz Simple syrup
- Ice
- 2 oz Tequila
- 3 Strawberries
- Club soda
- Lime slices for garnish

Instructions

1. In a tall glass, add the strawberries and mint. Pour in the simple syrup and muddle until flavors are released.

2. Add the ice. Pour the tequila over the ice. Mix gently.

3. Fill the rest of the glass with the club soda. Then garnish with mint leaves and strawberry.

Pomegranate mojito cocktail recipe

Are you looking for a holiday cocktail idea? This mojito recipe is enhanced with pomegranate, the holiday's favorite fruit. Drink it on New Year, Christmas, or anytime when you want to toast with family and friends.

Total time: 5 minutes

Servings: 1

Ingredients

- 2 oz. white rum
- 2 tsp. sugar
- 2 Tbsp. lime juice
- 10 fresh mint leaves
- 2 oz. pomegranate juice
- 3 oz. club soda
- 5-6 ice cubes
- 1-2 Tbsp. pomegranate seeds for garnish

Instructions

1. In a cocktail shaker, add the mint, sugar, rum, and lime juice. Shake well until the ingredients release their aroma and infuse together. It will take you about 15 seconds.

2. Pour into a serving glass. Add in the ice cubes.

3. Add the pomegranate juice and club soda. Stir using a bar spoon. Garnish with pomegranate seeds.

Summer watermelon mojito

If you were looking for a real summer cocktail to enhance your party, then this should be your pick. Why? Because nothing screams more "summer" than a glass of watermelon cocktail.

The sweet and refreshing taste will make you want more and more. This recipe will teach you how to prepare the perfect simple syrup that you can use for other cocktails too.

Total time: 20 minutes

Servings: 6

Ingredients

- Simple syrup:
- 1/2 cup water
- 20 leaves mint
- 1/2 cup granulated sugar
- Cocktail:
- 4 cups cubed seedless watermelon
- 2/3 cup freshly squeezed lime juice
- 1 cup white rum
- 1 1/2- 2 cups watermelon puree
- Optional garnishes: watermelon, limes, mint

Instructions

1. In a small saucepan, add the ingredients for the simple syrup. Bring the water to boil. Cook until the sugar is dissolved. Once done, remove it and let it cool.

2. Add the cubed watermelon into a blender or food processor. Pulse until pureed. Strain the puree to remove any solid particles.

3. Leave the watermelon puree in the fridge to chill.

4. In a large pitcher, add the rum, lime juice, puree, mint, and ⅔ of the simple syrup that you made. Mix and serve in glasses.

Refreshing raspberry mojito

Raspberries have a really strong flavor. That's why they can lift up any drink. Add them to your mojito, and you already have a winning combo. The secret trick is to make your own raspberry puree. This recipe will reveal how to do it.

Total time: 16 minutes

Servings: 1

Ingredients

For the puree:

- 1 cup of raspberries
- ¾ cup of sugar
- 1 cup of water

For the cocktail

- 3 fresh raspberries
- 2 ounces Raspberry Puree
- 2 ounces light rum
- 2 fresh mint leaves
- 3 ounces of soda water
- raspberries for garnish
- mint sprigs for garnish
- ice

Instructions

1. Add the raspberries, water, and sugar in a saucepan to prepare the puree. Cook for about 6 minutes or until thickened. Let it cool and strain through a sieve. Set aside.

2. In a tall glass, add the fresh raspberries and mint. Muddle until flavors are released.

3. Add some ice into the glass. Add whole raspberries and pour over the rum.

4. Add 2 oz of the raspberry puree. Fill the rest of the glass with soda water. Stir and serve.

Pina colada mojito

What happens when the two favorite summer cocktails are combined? You get this wonderful coconut and pineapple mojito recipe. All those tropical flavors are here to bring you the summer in a glass. Once you try it, you will certainly ask for more.

Total time: 10 minutes

Servings: 2

Ingredients

- 6 oz pineapple juice
- 2 tbsp lime juice
- 1/2 cup coconut water
- 4 oz rum
- 1/2 cup lime flavored sparkling water
- pineapple wedges, cherries for garnish

Instructions

1. In a cocktail shaker, add the coconut water, lime juice, rum, and pineapple juice.

2. Add ice into two tall glasses. Pour half of the cocktail mixture into each.

3. Pour ¼ cup club soda into each glass. Garnish and serve.

Alcohol-free virgin mojito

Do you want to offer an alcohol-free drink at the party? The Virgin Mojito is the perfect refreshing cocktail that doesn't contain any alcohol. If there are kids or pregnant women visiting your bar or party, then this will become a must. It is so refreshing and essential for the hot summer days.

Total time: 5 minutes

Servings: 1

Ingredients

- 10 mint leaves
- 2 tbsp honey simple syrup
- 2 tbsp lime juice
- sparkling water
- lime slices
- ice

Instructions

1. Add the mint leaves and lime juice in a tall glass. Muddle for one minute so that the mint will release its aroma.

2. Add the simple syrup. Also, add some ice.

3. Fill the rest with sparkling water. Decorate with lime slices and serve.

Vodka mojito

If you don't have rum by hand, then don't worry. This recipe will show you how to substitute it with vodka. Who knows, you might end up liking this version better than the original. In any case, this is a great twist to the classic recipe.

Total time: 3 minutes

Servings: 1

Ingredients

- 1/2 lime quartered
- 5 mint leaves
- 2 tbsp simple syrup
- 1.5 oz vodka
- 1/2 c club soda
- ice
- Lime slice
- Mint sprig

Instructions

1. Add the lime and mint in a tall glass. Muddle until the mint releases the aroma.

2. Pour in the vodka. Fill the glass with ice.

3. Pour in simple syrup. Then, add the club soda.

4. Stir gently with a bar spoon. Garnish with a lime slice and mint sprig.

Red mojito

Need a holiday drink that is a real crowd-pleaser? This red mojito will amaze everyone out there. The addition of cranberry will make it the perfect festive cocktail. Make a large batch and enjoy it with family and friends. Double the **Ingredients** and let the party begin!

Total time: 5 minutes

Servings: 3

Ingredients

- 1 cup cranberry juice
- 1 cup club soda
- 1/4 cup lime juice
- 6 oz light rum
- 1/3 c. mint leaves
- 2 tsp honey
- 3 c. ice
- lime slices
- Cranberries

Instructions

1. In a pitcher, combine the soda water, cranberry juice, mint, rum, lime juice, and honey. Mix well until combined.

2. Fill the glasses with the ice.

3. Divide the mixture evenly among the glasses. Garnish with lime and cranberries.

Frozen coconut mojito

Need a drink for a pool party? You can hold onto this amazing recipe. A frozen cocktail is everything that you need for a perfect summer. And this recipe will show you how to prepare frozen mojito with a hint of coconut. It will reveal one amazing secret, so be sure not to miss it!

Total time: 25 minutes

Servings: 4

Ingredients

- ½ cup of water
- ½ cup sugar
- 4 tbsp mint leaves (divided)
- ½ cup rum
- 14 oz coconut milk
- ½ cup coconut water
- 6 cups ice
- ¼ cup fresh squeezed lime juice

Instructions

1. In a small saucepan add sugar, water, and two tbsp of mint leaves. Bring to boil while stirring constantly. Cook for about 3 minutes or until the sugar is dissolved.

2. Remove the syrup from heat and strain it to remove the leaves. Set it aside to cool.

3. Once cooled, add the syrup into a blender. Add two tbsp of mint leaves, coconut milk, rum, lime juice, coconut water, and ice. Blend until smooth. Serve and enjoy!

Low carb mojito recipe

Do you need a cocktail that is low in carbs? Don't worry, because the perfect recipe does exist. This low carb mojito is as refreshing as the classic version. It is perfect for the people that mind their calorie and carb intake.

Total time: 10 minutes

Servings: 1

Ingredients

- 4 Leaves Mint
- 2 tbsp Lime Juice
- 2 packets Stevia or your preferred low-carb sweetener
- 1 1/2 ounce vodka
- 1/2 cup Club Soda
- Lime Slice to garnish
- Ice

Instructions

1. In a tall glass, add the mint leaves, lime juice, and stevia. Muddle until the aroma is released, and stevia or another sweetener is dissolved.

2. Fill the glass with ice. Pour in the vodka and club soda.

3. Top with lime wedges and mint.

Red vodka mojito

Preparing cocktails is pure art. But you have to know a few tips and tricks before you even start. This cocktail will reveal some secret methods for you. You will need to mix the vodka and juice in a shaker. Shake together with ice to chill your cocktail. Be sure to add the sparkling water in the end, so that it won't fizz when shaking.

Total time: 10 minutes

Servings: 2

Ingredients

- 3.5 ounces vodka
- 1/2 cup pomegranate blueberry juice
- 6 oz sparkling water
- 1 small splash of triple sec
- Seeds from 2 pomegranates
- 2 limes, sliced
- ice
- 1 handful of mint leaves

Instructions

1. Place the glasses in the fridge to chill. Remove and add in pomegranate seeds.

2. In a small mixing bowl, add the lime slices, triple sec, and mint. Muddle until the flavors are released.

3. In a cocktail shaker, add ice, vodka, and pomegranate blueberry juice. Shake well until the shaker is cold.

4. Divide the mixture between the two glasses. Add ice cubes and finish with sparkling water.

Green tea mojito

You can never have enough of mojito combinations. And this one will amaze you with the taste. The bitter green tea can add a kick of freshness and lift the cocktail. This recipe will impress all the green tea lovers out there. You can also prepare this recipe in a lither for a crowd. Multiply the **Ingredients** with the number of people that you want to serve.

Total time: 5 minutes

Servings:1

Ingredients

- 4 mint leaves
- 1 tbsp lime juice
- 2 tsp sugar
- 1/2 cup of brewed green tea, chilled
- 1 oz white rum

Instructions

1. In a tall glass, add sugar, mint, and lime juice. Muddle until the sugar is dissolved, and the flavors are released.

2. Fill ¾ of the glass with ice.

3. Pour in the rum and green tea. Stir with a bar spoon.

Summer peach mojito

This cocktail is a modern twist of the Cuban classic. It is perfect for the summer season when all you need is a refreshing glass of a good drink. Everyone will love the freshness and the sweet aromatic taste of the peach. So, don't skip this cocktail for your summer menu.

Total time: 5 minutes

Servings: 2

Ingredients

- 4 tbsp Fresh mint
- 4 peaches
- 4 oz white rum
- 2 tsp sugar
- Ice
- 4 oz club soda

Instructions

1. Slice two peaches and set them aside. You will need them for garnishing later.

2. Chop the remaining peaches. Add them into a cocktail shaker. Add the rum and sugar.

3. Muddle them until the sugar is dissolved and until well combined.

4. Divide the mixture among the two glasses.

5. Fill with ice and add peach slices. Top with club soda.

Italian Limoncello mojito

Limoncello is a famous Italian digestivo. It is a lemon-infused liquor with a sweet note. This makes it the perfect addition to cocktails. Mojito makes no exception for that. Prepare a limoncello mojito as a cool refreshment for any summer party.

Total time: 5 minutes

Servings: 1

Ingredients

- 1/2 lime, cut into wedges
- 1/5 oz simple syrup
- 2 tbsp Fresh mint
- Ice
- 2 oz limoncello or other lemon-flavored liquor
- Club soda

Instructions

1. In a tall glass, add lime wedges, simple syrup, and mint.

2. Muddle to combine the flavors.

3. Fill ¾ of the glass with ice. Pour the limoncello over the ice. Top with club soda and stir with a bar spoon.

Cherry lime mojito recipe

Preparing cocktails is all about creativity and finding alternative ways. If you don't feel like you want to muddle until the sugar is dissolved, you can always use simple syrup. It will bring sweetness without having pain in your hands. This trick will save you time too.

Total time: minutes

Servings:

Ingredients

- 6 cherries, pitted
- Freshly squeezed juice from 1 lime
- 12 mint leaves
- 2 oz white rum
- 2 oz simple syrup
- 1 cup crushed ice
- 1/2 cup club soda
- fresh cherry to garnish
- lime wedges to garnish
- mint leaves to garnish

Instructions

1. In a tall glass, add cherries, simple syrup, mint leaves, and rum.

2. Muddle to release the flavors and combine them.

3. Add the ice. Top with soda water and garnish.

Lavender lemonade mojito recipe

Lavender lemonade is many favorite summer drink. If you fuse it with a mojito, you will get an excellent cocktail. The combination of tastes will amaze everyone. The process of preparation is so easy so that anyone can do it. Follow this simple recipe and prepare the most refreshing summer cocktail.

Total time: 1 hour 15 minutes

Servings: 4

Ingredients

- Simple Syrup
- 1 cup of water
- 1 cup granulated sugar
- 1/4 cup dried lavender
- Cocktail
- 1 cup freshly squeezed lemon juice
- 2 cups of water
- 1 small bunch mint
- 1 cup light rum
- 3/4 cup lavender simple syrup, according to the recipe

Instructions

1. First, prepare the simple syrup. Put all the ingredients in a saucepan and bring to boil. Lower the temperature and let it simmer for 10 minutes. The syrup is ready when thickened. Turn off the heat and cover with a lid. Let it sit for one hour. Strain to remove the lavender. Let it cool in the fridge.

2. In a pitcher, add mint and lemon juice. Muddle until flavors are released. Add water, ¾ cup of the syrup that you prepared, and the rum. Stir.

3. Fill glasses with ice and serve.

Mojito sangria

Sangria is a famous Spanish drink made of wine and soda. What happens when you try to combine Sangria and mojito? This recipe will show you how to do it. Once you have a taste of the sweet and fizzy flavor, you will fall in love with this refreshing drink.

Total time: 10minutes

Servings:6

Ingredients

- 1/4 cup lime juice
- 1/2 cup simple syrup
- 20 mint leaves
- 1 cup white rum
- A bottle of sparkling white wine chilled
- 3 limes cut into wedges
- club soda

Instructions

1. In a mixing bowl, muddle the simple syrup and mint.

2. Add the muddles ingredients into a pitcher.

3. Add lime juice, limes, rum, and wine.

4. Add in some club soda right before serving. Serve in glasses filled with ice.

Frozen mojito with passion fruit

Mojitos are so fun to experiment with. This recipe will amaze every bartender or cocktail enthusiast out there. And it is something that you can sell at a higher price due to its uniqueness.

Total time: 5 minutes

Servings: 1

Ingredients

- 2 cups ice
- 1 oz Mint Syrup
- 2 oz white rum
- 2 oz Passion Fruit Mixer
- 1/2 lime, juiced
- 2 oz sparkling water
- mint leaves to garnish
- lime wedge to garnish

Instructions

1. Add the ice into a blender. Blend until the ice is crushed.

2. Fill the glass with the crushed ice.

3. Pour in rum, mixer, syrup, club soda, and lime juice. Mix well.

4. Add more ice on top of the glass.

5. Garnish with mint and lime.

Watermelon mojito popsicles

Popsicles are kids' favorite. But adults can also enjoy them during the summer. This recipe will show you how to prepare a batch of refreshing summer popsicles, infused with alcohol. The summer heat was no match for these watermelon popsicles!

Total time: 5 hours

Servings: 10

Ingredients

- 3 cups Watermelon, cut in cubes
- 4 oz Lemon Juice
- 4 oz Simple Syrup
- 5 oz White Rum
- 12 large mint leaves, rough chopped

Instructions

1. Add all the ingredients into a blender, pulse until the mixture is well combined and smooth.

2. Pour the popsicle mixture into molds and add sticks.

3. Freeze the mojito treats for a few hours. Run the mold under water to easily remove them.

Refreshing blackberry mojito popsicles

Craving for an icy treat with a touch of booze? This recipe will show you how to prepare frozen mojito popsicles with blackberry. The intense flavor of the fruit will dominate, and it guarantees a full pleasure.

Total time: 4 hours

Servings: 8

Ingredients

- 1 cup fresh mint leaves
- 2 cups blackberries
- 1/4 cup sugar
- 1/3 cup white rum
- 1/4 cup fresh lime juice

Instructions

1. In a blender, add all of the ingredients for your blackberry mojito popsicles, except for the rum. Pulse until everything is combined and smooth.

2. Strain the mixture to remove the blackberry seeds.

3. Add the rum into the strained mixture and mix well.

4. Pour into popsicle molds and freeze for at least 4 hours.

Strawberry mojito popsicles

If the other recipes weren't enough, here is a strawberry popsicle recipe. It is really helpful when you have so many different variations to experiment with. Keep in mind that not all fruits go well with mint. But strawberry is an exception.

Total time: 5 hours minutes

Servings: 8

Ingredients

- 5 strawberries, sliced
- 1 lime, juiced
- 12 mint leaves
- 3 cups of strawberry lemonade
- 3/4 cup rum
- 2 tbsp of simple syrup

Instructions

1. In a bowl, mix the lime juice, lemonade, and rum. Stir well.

2. Add the sliced strawberries and mint into the popsicle molds.

3. Pour the mixture in the molds. Pop them in the freezer for about 5 hours.

Easy kiwi mojito popsicles

Kiwi, mint, and rum is another winning combination. You will love the sweet and sour flavor, infused by the rum. You will need only three ingredients to make this recipe. So, let's get started!

Total time: 5 hours

Servings:6

Ingredients

- 8 kiwis, peeled
- 1 3/4 cup limeade
- 1/2 cup mint leaves

Instructions

1. In a blender, add kiwis cut in half, and the mint leaves. Blend until smooth and well combined.

2. Add into a bowl. Pour in the limeade and stir well.

3. Divide the mixture evenly among the popsicle molds. Freeze for about 5 hours.

Coconut mojito popsicles

Are you looking for a creamy and tropical popsicle, with a hint of your favorite summer cocktail? This coconut mojito popsicle recipe is here to satisfy all your cravings. Once you taste it, it will become your all-time favorite. Prepare a large batch for a summer party or a pool party.

Total time: 6 hours

Servings: 5

Ingredients

- 13.5 oz full-fat coconut milk
- ¼ cup packed fresh mint leaves
- ¼ cup maple syrup
- zest of 1 lime
- 1 vanilla bean
- 1 tbsp lime juice
- 2 tbsp rum

Instructions

1. Add maple syrup, coconut milk, mint, lime juice, and lime zest into a small saucepan.

2. Scrape out the seeds from the vanilla bean. Add the bean and the seeds into the saucepan.

3. Cook over medium heat from 2 to 4 minutes. Remove from heat and let it rest for half an hour.

4. Strain the mixture through a sieve to remove the leaves and bean.

5. Add in the rum.

6. Pour the mixture into popsicle molds. Freeze for around 5 hours or until solid.

Frozen mojito slushie

When the summer heat strikes, it is time for a refreshing slushie. Add a hint of mojito in it, and your favorite summer drink is ready. All you need is four ingredients and 5 minutes of your time.

Total time: 5 minutes

Servings: 4

Ingredients

- 16 oz lime sorbet
- 8 shots light rum
- 1 tray ice cubes
- 1/2 cup mint leaves

Instructions

1. In a blender, add half of the ingredients for your mojito slushie. Pulse until combined. Blend on high until smooth.

2. Serve in two glasses.

3. Repeat with the rest of the ingredients and serve. If you have a large blender, you can do it all at once.

Alcohol-free watermelon mojito slushie

Here is another refreshing recipe for children or people that don't consume alcohol. The combination of lime, mint, and watermelon is a match made in heaven. This slushie will take all of your gatherings to the next level.

Total time: 20 minutes

Servings: 3

Ingredients

- 1/4 cup freshly squeezed Lime Juice
- 1/4 Whole Seedless Watermelon
- 15 mint leaves

Instructions

1. Chop the watermelon to chunks. Place it in the blender. Puree until smooth.

2. Add in the lime juice into the blender. Add in the mint leaves too.

3. Blend again. Let it chill in the fridge for 10 minutes. Serve and enjoy!

Conclusion

After checking these recipes, we are sure that you already found the thing that you were looking for.

This recipe book will become your staple when it comes to parties or even reviving your business. It is definitely a must for all the people that are after good cocktails. The mojito is an excellent drink in its original form and all its variations.

Now, you know the secret trick behind preparing the original and authentic Cuban mojito recipe. You also learned a helpful shortcut. If your hands hurt from the muddling and trying to dissolve the sugar, go for simple syrup. If you need to prepare your special mojito recipe in a cocktail mixer, be sure to add the club soda in the end. These are the tricks that will stay on your mind, thanks to this Mojito Recipe Book.

Now it is up to you to go out there and impress everyone with your new mojito recipes. All of the guests will be impressed with the taste and different variations.

Feel free to conquer the world of cocktails with your favorite recipe book!

About the Author

Nancy Silverman is an accomplished chef from Essex, Vermont. Armed with her degree in Nutrition and Food Sciences from the University of Vermont, Nancy has excelled at creating e-books that contain healthy and delicious meals that anyone can make and everyone can enjoy. She improved her cooking skills at the New England Culinary Institute in Montpelier Vermont and she has been working at perfecting her culinary style since graduation. She claims that her life's work is always a work in progress and she only hopes to be an inspiration to aspiring chefs everywhere.

Her greatest joy is cooking in her modern kitchen with her family and creating inspiring and delicious meals. She often says that she has perfected her signature dishes based on her family's critique of each and every one.

Nancy has her own catering company and has also been fortunate enough to be head chef at some of Vermont's most exclusive restaurants. When a friend suggested she share some of her outstanding signature dishes, she decided to add cookbook author to her repertoire of personal achievements. Being a technological savvy woman, she felt the e-book realm would be a better fit and soon she had her first cookbook available online. As of today, Nancy has sold over 1,000 e-books and has shared her culinary experiences and brilliant recipes with people from all over the world! She plans on expanding into self-help books and dietary cookbooks, so stayed tuned!

Author's Afterthoughts

Thank you for making the decision to invest in one of my cookbooks! I cherish all my readers and hope you find joy in preparing these meals as I have.

There are so many books available and I am truly grateful that you decided to buy this one and follow it from beginning to end.

I love hearing from my readers on what they thought of this book and any value they received from reading it. As a personal favor, I would appreciate any feedback you can give in the form of a review on Amazon and please be honest! This kind of support will help others make an informed choice on and will help me tremendously in producing the best quality books possible.

My most heartfelt thanks,

Nancy Silverman

If you're interested in more of my books, be sure to follow my author page on Amazon (can be found on the link Bellow) or scan the QR-Code.

https://www.amazon.com/author/nancy-silverman

Printed in Great Britain
by Amazon